DA | | Yossel Zissel and the wisdor
| | SC J SCH

Schwartz, Amy.
        Hillel Torah Day School

P9-DGB-683

J E   J-91-82
S   c.1

Schwartz, Amy

Yossel Zissel and the Wisdom of Chelm.

LIBRARY
HILLEL TORAH
NORTH SUBURBAN DAY SCHOOL
7120 LARAMIE AVENUE
SKOKIE, ILLINOIS 60077

Yossel Zissel
and the
Wisdom of Chelm

WRITTEN AND ILLUSTRATED BY

Amy Schwartz

LIBRARY
HILLEL TORAH
NORTH SUBURBAN DAY SCHOOL
7120 LARAMIE AVENUE
SKOKIE, ILLINOIS 60077

DISCARDED

THE JEWISH PUBLICATION SOCIETY

Philadelphia · New York · Jerusalem   5746 · 1986

JE
S
c.1   J-91-82

For Laura

Copyright © 1986 by Amy Schwartz
All rights reserved   First edition
Manufactured in the United States of America
Library of Congress Cataloging in Publication Data

Schwartz, Amy.
  Yossel Zissel and the wisdom of Chelm.

  Summary: Relates how Yossel Zissel, butcher of Chelm,
goes to Warsaw to collect a fortune in gold inherited
from his uncle and returns to Chelm empty-handed.
  [1. Humorous stories]   I. Title.
PZ7.S406Yo   1986   [Fic]   85-24024
ISBN 0-8276-0258-8

Designed by Adrianne Onderdonk Dudden

Some have said that Chelm was a town of fools. But any true friend of Chelm will tell you that this is not true.

"Perhaps sometimes foolish things happened *to* Chelmites," he would say. "But the Chelmites themselves were the wisest people in the world!

"Take Yossel Zissel the butcher, for example.

"Yossel Zissel was so wise that in the winter he wore his boots on his ears so that he wouldn't make footprints in the snow.

"He was so wise that on Passover he nailed the matzo balls to the plates so that they wouldn't roll off.

"In fact, we have Yossel Zissel to thank for the wisdom of Chelm that exists throughout the world today!"

This is how it happened.

One day, while Yossel Zissel was butchering a chicken, a letter came for him. It said:

Dear Yossel Zissel, Your Uncle Pinya has died in Warsaw. He has left his entire life's savings to you to share with the people of Chelm.

Yossel Zissel set out immediately to claim his fortune.

As Yossel Zissel traveled, he thought of the wonders the money would buy.

"I'll build a wall around Chelm to keep out the cold!

"I'll buy thousands of bagel holes for Berel the baker!"

Yossel Zissel's heart was filled with joy.

In Warsaw, Yossel Zissel quickly found the house of Uncle Pinya's lawyer.

The lawyer took a big key from around his neck and unlocked a back room. Yossel Zissel could not believe his eyes. The room was filled with bags and bags of gold.

"All this is yours," the lawyer said. "My servants will help you carry it back to Chelm."

"Oh, no," Yossel Zissel said. "I carried myself here, and I'm a man of over two hundred pounds! I can carry the gold by myself, too."

Yossel Zissel left Warsaw with a bounce in his step. But as the sun rose higher in the sky, the bags grew heavier and heavier. Yossel Zissel walked slower and slower.

"Oy! My poor legs!" Yossel Zissel groaned. "My aching back!"

And when the sun set, Yossel Zissel began hearing noises in the bushes.

"Thieves! They'll want my gold!" Yossel Zissel trembled.

"They'll want my life!" Sweat ran down Yossel Zissel's brow.

At last Yossel Zissel stumbled into an inn. He told his worries to the innkeeper.

"Here's what you should do," the innkeeper said. "Trade me your biggest bag of gold for my donkey. Thieves won't want an old donkey! And the donkey will carry you and your gold on his back. You'll ride like the czar!"

This idea appealed to Yossel Zissel. But, remember, Yossel Zissel was a very wise man.

"If trading one bag of gold for one animal is a good idea," he said to himself, "then trading all my bags of gold for lots of animals is an even better idea!"

So in the morning Yossel Zissel traded the innkeeper his biggest bag of gold for the innkeeper's old donkey. Then Yossel Zissel did business with the other guests at the inn.

He traded away all his gold for chickens, goats, sheep, and cows.

And, once again, he headed down the road to Chelm.

"Let me think," Yossel Zissel said to himself as he wearily sat down under a tree. "The gold was too heavy, but these animals are nothing but trouble. I need to trade them for something light and easy to carry."

A feather drifted down from a chicken that was perched on Yossel Zissel's head.

"That's it!" Yossel Zissel exclaimed. "Feathers! What could be lighter than a feather?" Happily, Yossel Zissel fell asleep.

Yossel Zissel's chickens ran into every bush along the road. His goats nibbled every blade of grass.

The sheep walked too fast, and the donkey walked too slowly. By nightfall Yossel Zissel had traveled only half a mile.

LIBRARY
HILLEL TORAH
NORTH SUBURBAN DAY SCHOOL
7120 LARAMIE AVENUE
SKOKIE, ILLINOIS 60077

When he awoke, Yossel Zissel rounded up his animals and herded them into the center of a nearby village. He drove them into the town hall, and asked the mayor, "Will you give me feathers for my animals?"

The mayor looked at Yossel Zissel's chickens, goats, cows, and sheep. He saw eggs, milk, and wool coats for his village. "Certainly!" the mayor said. "My townspeople will be happy to make the trade."

The villagers gathered in front of the town hall. A woman traded Yossel Zissel a feather pillow for two chickens. A man traded a feather bed for Yossel Zissel's donkey. By evening Yossel Zissel had traded away all his animals. He was a happy man.

But when Yossel Zissel turned to look at his new fortune, his smile disappeared. One feather is very light. But the feathers from a whole town, that is another thing.

"What am I to do?" Yossel Zissel groaned.

Just then a breeze ruffled Yossel Zissel's hair, and he had an idea. "Feathers float easily on the wind," he said. "And winds blow into Chelm all the time. I know just what to do!"

The next breeze was blowing toward Chelm. Yossel Zissel ran from pillow to pillow and from feather bed to feather bed. He slit them all open with his knife.

The sky became white with feathers and then became a deep blue again as the feathers blew toward Chelm.

Yossel Zissel did not sleep at all that night. He ran as fast as feathers fly on a breeze. He ran all night and all the next day until he was back in his beloved Chelm.

"Hello, friends! Anything new?" he asked the Chelmites, looking around for his feathers.

"Welcome back, Yossel Zissel! Anything new with *you*?" The Chelmites wondered where Yossel Zissel had hidden his bags of gold.

But there were no feathers in Chelm and no bags of gold. Yossel Zissel told the Chelmites the story of his journey.

"I'm sure the feathers will be along any day," he said. "We just have to be patient."

The Chelmites were patient for days. They were patient for weeks. They carried bags about with them and put buckets on their heads to catch the returning feathers. But the bags and buckets remained empty.

Yossel Zissel began to have trouble sleeping.

One night Yossel Zissel did sleep, and he had a dream. He dreamed he was flying over the world on a feather.

Yossel Zissel sat up in bed. He put on his boots and ran out of his house. He ran from door to door.

"It is not a misfortune that our feathers have not returned," he said to his neighbors. "Rather, it is an omen. God has given us a sign.

"Just as our feathers are now traveling to the four corners of the world, it is time for us to travel also.

"We have been selfish. It is time to share the wisdom of Chelm with the rest of the world."

The Chelmites agreed that Yossel Zissel was right, as he always was. They packed up their belongings.

And, with Yossel Zissel leading the way, they left Chelm to seek their fortunes. The Chelmites settled among the peoples of the world. They made new homes and raised many sons and daughters.

So, if you have noticed yourself acting like a Chelmite at times, well, maybe your great-great-great-grandfather or your great-great-great-grandmother was among those who, that night, followed Yossel Zissel out of Chelm.

LIBRARY
HILLEL TORAH
NORTH SUBURBAN DAY SCHOOL
7120 LARAMIE AVENUE
SKOKIE, ILLINOIS 60077

**LIBRARY
HILLEL TORAH
NORTH SUBURBAN DAY SCHOOL
7120 LARAMIE AVENUE
SKOKIE, ILLINOIS 60077**